Typesetting a Manuscript for Printing with Word

How prepare your manuscript for self-publishing with professional looking results

Eddie Snipes

ISBN 978-1475000924

GES Book Publishing
Carrollton, GA

Published by GES Book Publishing
Copyright © 2012 by Eddie Snipes
and
GES Book Publishing

Cover Design by Eddie Snipes

What is typesetting?

Typesetting is to lay out the chapters, fonts, headings, and justifying the text so that it is readable and professional looking when printed as a book.

Microsoft Word can be frustrating. I know. That's stating the obvious, but how much more true this is when formatting headers and footers. I decided to write this article because of how difficult it was to find relevant information. It seemed like there were sites that gave partial information or settings for business documents, but I wasn't able to find an easy to follow method for formatting a manuscript for printing.

In this series of articles, I am going to take you step by step on how to format a professional looking manuscript for printing. This should be helpful for independent authors who want to use sources like Create Space or Lightning Source. We want our book's layout to be indistinguishable from the rest of the industry. A cheap looking book will be treated as such.

There are professional typesetting software applications that make setup easy, but these are very costly and not practical for independent authors. Some articles I found stated that it is impossible to create a proper manuscript using Word, but this is not the case at all. My first book, I Called Him Dancer, was formatted in Word and people are amazed when they find out it was typeset with this 'inferior' Word program. There are some types of books that don't format well in Word, but for the average book, you can customize a professional looking manuscript that is no different in appearance than a professionally typeset one.

By the end of this series of articles, I will have walked you through typesetting your work from beginning to end. It isn't especially difficult. The problem is that Word isn't intuitive. It's hard to know where to go in order to do what you want. Once you find the right place to click, the setup is easy.

This series of articles will begin with customizing footers for your book.

Setting Footers on your manuscript

This topic also applies to setting headers.

When setting up a manuscript, it's usually necessary to have the footer change for each section. At a minimum, you want to have a separate footer that begins at the first chapter. You do not want the title page (or pages) to have numbers and footer information. It makes the manuscript look unprofessional.

Let me first define headers and footers. If you're new to Word, this may not be familiar to you. A header is the information printed in the margins at the top of the page, and a footer is the information printed at the bottom of the page. Normally, this information will contain the page number and the chapter title. Some books may also include the book title. In this article, I'll be using the footer since this is the format I prefer. But the exact same methods apply to headers.

Planning your footers.

Decide how you want your footers to display. If you want the same footer throughout the book, you will only need two sections. If you want to have a footer that is unique for each chapter, you'll need to create section breaks at the end of each chapter. This will make the next chapter part of a new section.

To create a section break, go to the end of the last sentence, or the beginning of the title of the next chapter.

Click on the Page Layout Tab, click Breaks, then choose Next Page in the section break option. See below:

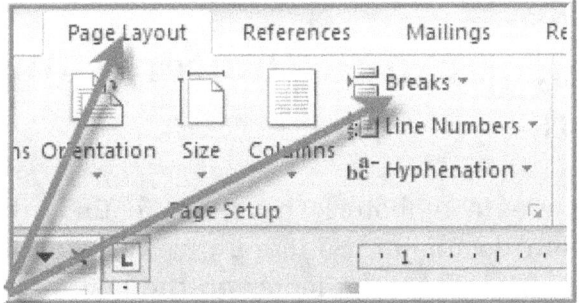

A section break is an invisible field and will act the same as a standard page break. You can see what these breaks look like by revealing the formatting. To do this, click on the paragraph symbol on the home tab.

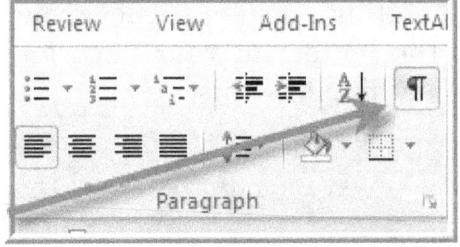

When formatting is revealed, the section break will look like the image below:

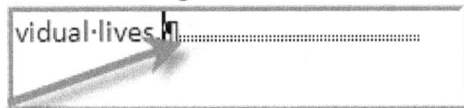

The paragraph symbol indicates a carriage return. The dotted lines indicate a section break. A page break will be symbolized with a single dotted line.

A **page break** serves just as the name indicates. It forces a new page so that the next piece of information begins on a new page. The **section break** will also create a new page, but it treats each page within the section as a logically separated block of text. To the reader, these two options don't look different, but when it comes to formatting, section breaks serve a very important function.

Customizing unique footers for each section.

By default, if you create a footer, the same footer will show throughout your document. So if you put 'Chapter 1' in the footer of your first page, the footer on the last page will still say 'Chapter 1' - regardless of what chapter you're in. To separate chapters, you'll need to break the link between sections.

To break the section link, go into the footer editing mode. The easiest way to get into editing mode is to move your curser into the margin at the bottom of your page and double click. You will see something like this:

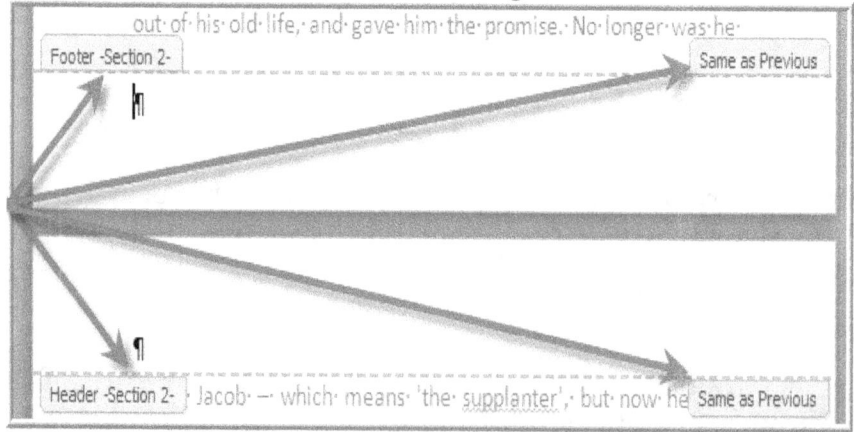

The tab indicates which section you are in. If you have a title page, it should be section 1. Chapter 1 will be section 2, and so on.

Take note of the right-hand tab. This lets you know that this header or footer will pull its information from the previous section. Since this is Section 2, anything in footer of section 1 will show up in these fields.

If section 1 is the title page, you want it to be blank. This makes section 2 blank. However, if you break the link between sections 1 and 2 and put information in the footer, such as 'Chapter 1', then Section 3 will also hold this same information.

If you're going to have a customized formating, such as the chapter name and page number, I recommend customizing the first chapter, and then break the sections up. This way you'll only have to rename each chapter and won't have to customize the formatting and numbers from scratch for each chapter. This will all make sense when we start editing the footers.

Let's begin by breaking the link between Section 2 from Section 1. Section 1 is the title pages, so it won't have numbering or footers. We want it to be blank.

While in the footer editing mode, look at the top of the screen. You should already be under the tab titled 'Design'. See below:

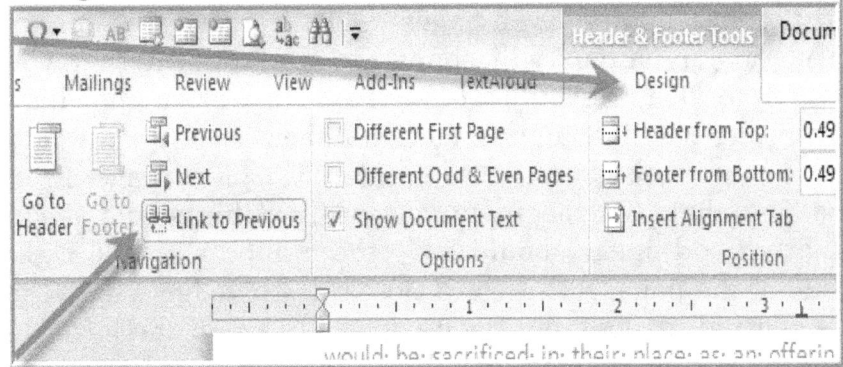

If you don't see this, make sure you are in the footer editing mode by doubl-clicking near the bottom of the page.

To break the link between your current section and the previous section, click on the highlighted area as shown above, 'Link to Previous'. This will break your link from section 1 to section 2, but anything below section 2 will remain linked.

Once you click to break the link, the 'Same as Previous' tab will disappear from the box around the footer. Now we are ready to format our chapter footers.

In this example, I'm going to use my chapter names and add page numberings. In order to look more professional, I want my even numbers to appear on the left of the page, and my odd numbers to appear on the right. This will make the printed page number to always be on the outside edge of the book for easy viewing. We don't want the numbers to be near the binding where they are hard to see.

In the image above, there is a checkbox that says, 'Different Odd and Even pages'. Click to check this option. Your footer banner will change to indicate whether you are on an odd or even page. My first chapter begins on an even page, so I want my page number to be on the left. Since the book cover isn't considered a page, page 1, an odd number, will begin to your right. This would mean that all odd pages should have the numbers on the right side of the page, so they are closest to the edge where the reader will be looking. Even pages will be on the left side of the book, so the page numbers should always be printed on the left side of even pages.

Note: Some versions of word will re-enable the link to previous section if you change to odd/even footers. You may need to break the link between section 1 and 2 again. It's not a big issue. Just click the 'Link to Previous' option again when you're ready to break the link.

Also Note: You will need to break the link on the first odd page footer in the new section you are editing, *and* you'll need to break the link to previous on the first even page in the section you are editing. If you forget to break the link *before* making changes, you'll have to go back and edit the previous section again. Whatever you type into the footers will populate all the footers in that section, and all linked sections. The same is true for headers.

We are on an even page, so the cursor should be on the left side of the footer. If not, under the design tab, click on 'Insert Alignment' and choose 'left'.

Next, insert a page number. Click on the page number icon on the upper right of your menu (see below).

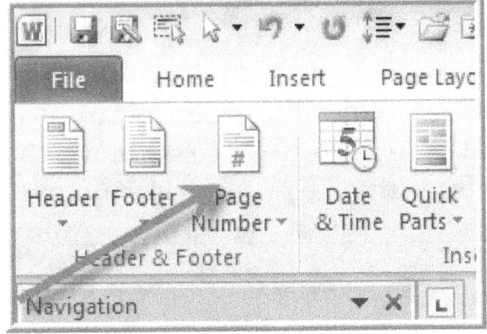

From the drop-down option, select 'Current Position'. This will put the page number where your cursor is and make formatting much easier.

I like simple numbers, so I clicked on plain number.

The next thing I want is for my chapter name to appear on the right side of the page. To do this, click on Insert Alignment option – see below:

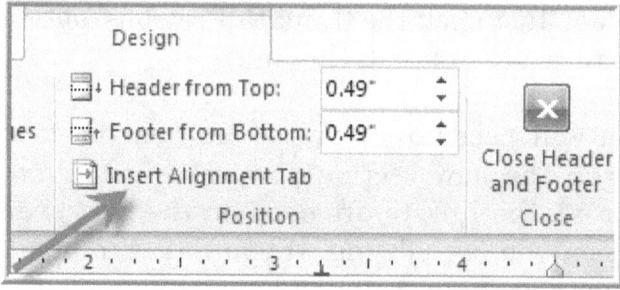

Choose 'Right' and click OK.
This moves your cursor to the right of the field.

Type in any text you like. Since I want the chapter name to appear, I'll be typing in the title of each chapter.

Now all your even pages should have footers, but your odd pages will have blank footers. If you didn't select the option to have different odd and even pages, then all your footers will be populated with the same formatting and position.

To populate the odd footers, follow the same process as with the even footers, but insert the title first, move the cursor to the right and insert the page number. *Be sure and choose Current Position when selecting a page number option.*

Now if you scroll down, each page will have odd page numbers to the right and even numbers to the left. The title needs to be on the opposite side of the page.

Changing Chapter Names.

Since we didn't break the link between sections, all the sections will have the correct numbering, but also the same chapter name. This creates a template for your chapters, but you'll need to change the chapter names. This will be quick now that you have completed your formatting. The first step is to break the link between sections.

Move to the next chapter and go into the footer. If the section number doesn't change, then you haven't created a section break for that chapter. Be aware that if you make a change anywhere in a section, every page will be altered. That means if you are missing a section break and you edit the footer, you will have to go back and fix it after adding a section break.

If you see the tab, 'Same as Previous', Click on the option 'Link to Previous' to break it.

You only have to change the footer once per section. When you make a change to the even pages, all the even pages below it will be changed. The same is true for odd pages.

Do this for each chapter and your manuscript will have a professional style footing that will help readers find the right page and know what chapter they are in. Some authors like to put the title of the book in the header. The process for formatting the header is the same as the footer.

If you've followed these steps, the title page will not have a footer, and each page thereafter will be properly formatted.

Text Formatting

Configuring Word

Before formatting the text, it's important to configure Word with only the features necessary for your book. Fortunately, with word, you can make as many changes as you want and have them ONLY apply to the document you are using. When making a change in Options, you'll see something like the image below:

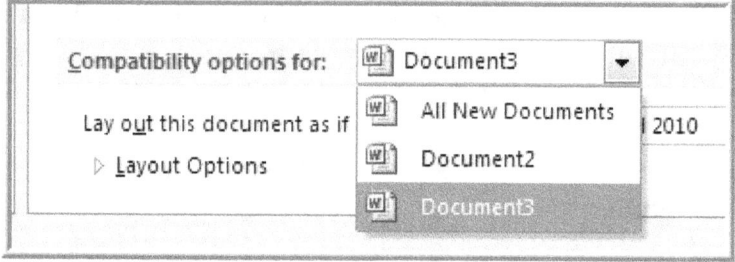

I have two new documents open. I can apply my change to my current document (which is the default action), another open document, or I can apply this to all new documents. Unless you're making a change you want to apply to every document, leave your current document as the default option.

One thing I highly recommend is to strip away all downward compatibility options. To do this, go to File, Options, click advanced, and scroll down to compatibility options. Click the '**Lay out as if created in'**: and choose the version of word you are using. In my case, I have Windows 2010.

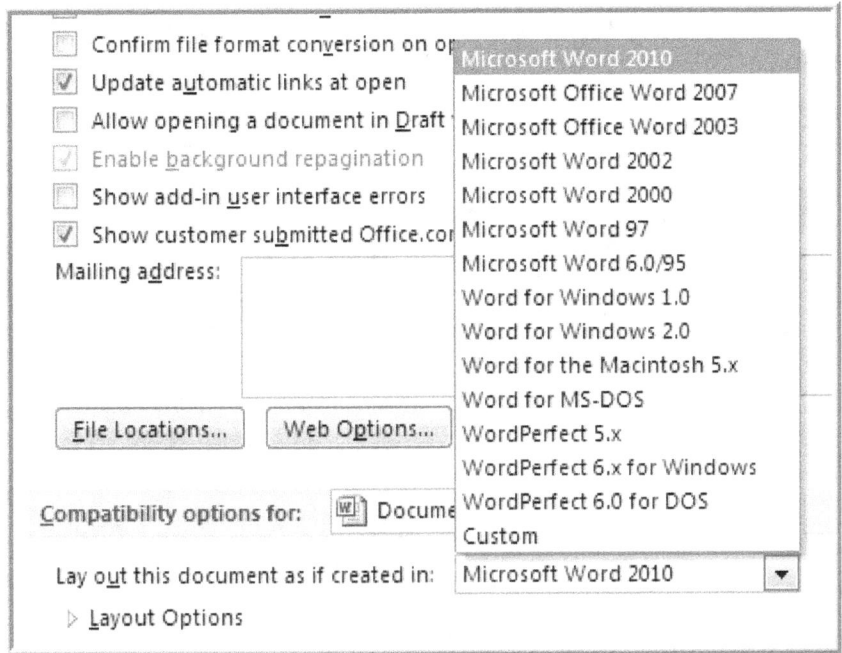

The downward compatibility options enables features that allows your document to be functional in an older version of Word. This won't be necessary for typesetting. The finished product will be saved as an Adobe PDF document, so there will be no need for compatibility with other word processing applications.

To make a book printed page look good, the text will have to be justified. Word has a tendency of stretching the text when trying to fill up a line. Though newer versions have improved in this area, the Word Perfect Style of justification is much better for typesetting. Word allows this option, but it is buried out of site. To enable **Word Perfect justification**, click on File, Click Options, then click Advanced. Scroll to the very bottom and you'll see Compatibility Options.

Click the arrow to expand in order to reveal the various setting options. Scroll to the 'D's' and you'll see '**Do full**

justification the way WordPerfect 6.x for Windows does'. Check this option as shown below:

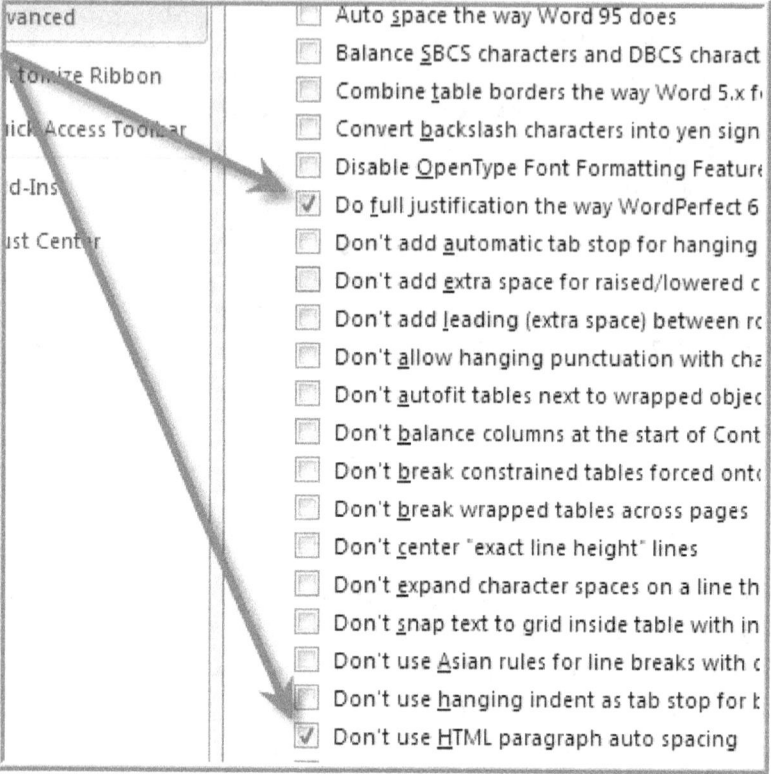

While you're in this area, also check the box, 'Don't use HTML paragraph auto spacing'. This formatting option can produce unexpected results.

One last option you should turn off is, 'Use Printer Metrics to layout document.' Uncheck this box. This option can alter the layout based on the printer's driver your computer uses. Since this is not going to be printed with a personal computer, this should not be used. It can cause the document to look one way on your computer, but different when printed in book format.

From this point on, formatting is an easy task.

Text Formatting

Embedding Fonts

It's always a good idea to embed the fonts you are using when preparing a document for printing. If the font is not embedded, the printer will substitute the closest compatible font, but this can alter the look of your manuscript. Embedding will avoid this problem. I'll mention this later when it's time to create the pdf, but let's get familiarized with this now.

To embed, click on file, options, Save and then scroll to the bottom of the window. Below '**Preserve fidelity when sharing this document**', click **Embed fonts in the file**. See below:

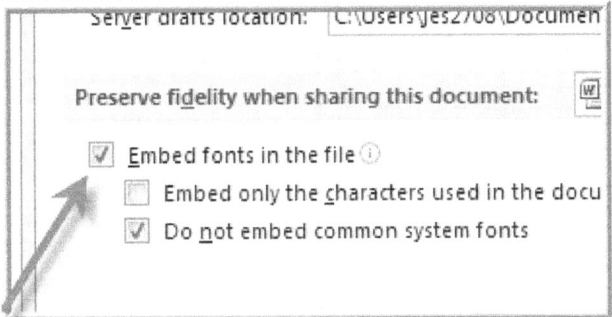

Embedding fonts greatly enlarges the file size, so to save space, you may want to check the option to not embed common system fonts. It also won't hurt to leave this unchecked.

When you go to save the manuscript as a PDF file, DO NOT print to a PDF file. This will not preserve your fonts. Instead, click on File, Save As, and choose .pdf as your file type.

Formatting the text

Depending on how you put your book together, you might have various fonts. I cut and paste from another application, and sometimes it creates a mixture of fonts. Try not to have more than one font in your final document. In rare cases, you may want to use a second one, but the less fonts the better.

To make sure your entire document has only one style of font, follow these steps.
Press Ctrl-A. This will highlight all the text in the document.
Now select a font. Choose a font that looks good in print. Times New Roman isn't as readable in book format as some of the other fonts. I prefer Calibri or Century Schoolbook. These format well and look good in print, but feel free to use what fits your book.

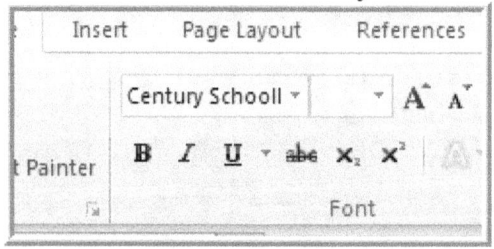

Leave the font size blank. This is important because any headings or formatted text will be changed and will produce undesireable results. If you have mixed font sizes, you may have to manually change them where needed.

Aligning the Title Page

The title page should be centered. Press Ctrl-Home. This will take your cursor to the very top of the document. Hold down the shift key and press the down arrow. Press it until you get to the bottom of the title page.

With the text highlighted, Click the Center Alignment icon. You can find this on the Home tab on the Word menu. See Below:

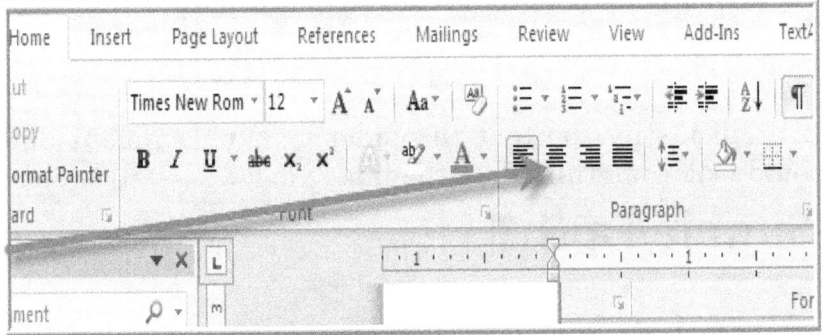

Justifying the Body.

Move your cursor to the beginning of chapter 1. Make sure the cursor is in front of the first letter of text. See below:

Simple·Faith¶

The·Apostle·Paul·wrote·to·the·Corinthian·church·and· expressed·his·fear·that·they·might·be·drifting·away·from·the· simplicity·of·their·faith·in·Christ.·The·same·threat·faces·you,·your· church,·and·every·Christian·on·a·daily·basis.·If·we·allow·human· philosophy·to·muddy·the·waters·of·truth,·nothing·will·be·clear.¶

I·once·had·a·discussion·with·someone·about·faith.·In·our· talk,·it·was·stated·that·faith·was·too·complicated·to·understand.· Books·on·theology·and·Christian·philosophy·clouded·the·issue·and· made·things·seem·too·hard·to·grasp·by·anyone·other·than·learned· scholars.·Once·again,·I·pointed· back·to·the·simplicity·of·the· gospel.·The·Bible·says,·"Abraham·believed·God,·and·his·faith·was· accounted·to·him·for·righteousness."¶

Now hold down the Shift and Control keys and while holding, press the key labelled 'End'. This will highlight all the text from your cursor until the end of the manuscript. Now press the Justify icon.

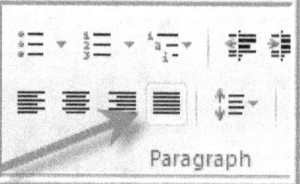

This will justify the text throughout your document and should look something like the image below:

Simple·Faith¶

The· Apostle· Paul· wrote· to· the· Corinthian· church· and· expressed· his· fear· that· they· might· be· drifting· away· from· the· simplicity·of·their·faith·in·Christ.·The·same·threat·faces·you,·your· church,· and· every· Christian· on· a· daily· basis.· If· we· allow· human· philosophy· to·muddy·the·waters·of·truth,·nothing·will·be·clear.¶

I· once· had· a· discussion· with· someone· about· faith.· In· our· talk,· it· was· stated· that· faith· was· too· complicated·to·understand.· Books·on·theology·and·Christian·philosophy·clouded·the·issue·and· made·things·seem·too·hard·to·grasp·by·anyone·other·than·learned· scholars.· Once· again,· I· pointed· back· to· the· simplicity· of· the· gospel .·The·Bible·says ·"Abraham·believed·God ·and·his·faith·was·

The jagged look of the text has been replaced with neatly aligned paragraphs.

The paragraph symbol at the end of my paragraphs are from the formatting codes. They will not print and can be turned on or off by clicking the paragraph symbol on the main tab of the Word menu.

To verify that the paragraphs look good, browse through your manuscript and look for any stretched out text. Odd looking paragraphs can be resolved by hyphinating words, adding or subtracting a word, or tweaking the text. Small blocks of indented text, such as quotes, can misformat. It might be helpful to leave these unjustified. To remove justification, highlight the text and click the alignment icon you prefer using.

You'll need to play around to resolve any issues, though there should be few – if any. Turning on the Word Perfect formatting resolves most odd paragraphs.

If you have a word that is too stretched out, or several lines that are stretched, you can manually tweak the justification. To do this, highlight the text you want to adjust. Under the Home tab, click to expand the Font options, go to the Advanced tab, and choose to condense the text. See below:

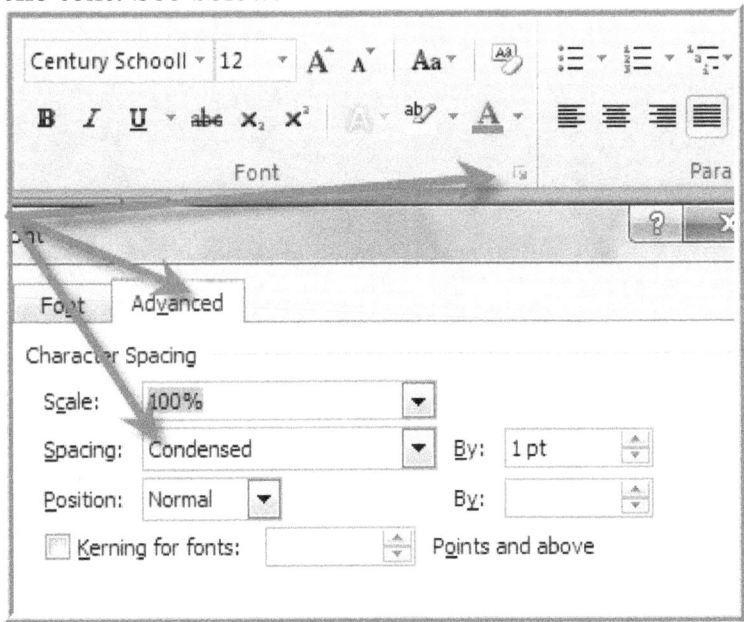

If you're trying to fill in a little text, you can also expand a word or block of text. Some or all of the text can be returned to normal if it looks odd.

If your manuscript has an index or other addition at the end of the book, you may want to leave these out of your justification and align them separately.

Once completed, the look and feel of your manuscript text should be book-ready. Now all you need is a good table of contents and to set up the page layout.

Text Formatting

Building a Table of Contents

Whether your book is fiction or non-fiction, it needs a table of contents. Aside from the fact that readers need it to locate the chapter they want, a book with a table of contents looks more professional, and readers can browse the contents to get an idea of what to expect from your book.

Word users have an easy path to creating a table of contents, but it does take a little preparation.

Let's first talk about what we expect our table of contents to display. If your book is fiction, most likely the only information needed is the chapter name and page number. If it's non-fiction, you'll need to decide how much information the reader needs in order to find the right chapter and subtopic.

Unless your book is a technical manual, most likely you won't need more than two levels. Beyond two levels, the contents begin to look crowded. If the content of your non-fiction book is well identified by the chapter name, then stick with one level. However, if your topic has a lot of subtopics, give the reader a few levels in which to find the subtopic they want.

For example, suppose your book is on gardening. One chapter may be on vegetables, one on flowers, trees, composting, etc. Under vegetables, having subtopics in the table of contents on potatoes, tomatoes, beans and other plants would be helpful. But having subtopics under beans would be cumbersome. The chapter may have additional subtopics, but the table of contents probably should not. Of course, that's my opinion, so you may want to do it your way.

Consider these things while planning your table of contents. You'll need to know how much you want to present to the reader in a moment.

Headings.

Headings and headers are not the same thing. We looked at headers when looking at the header and footer options. Headings refers to how the text in the body of your document is formatted. Below is a list of common headings:

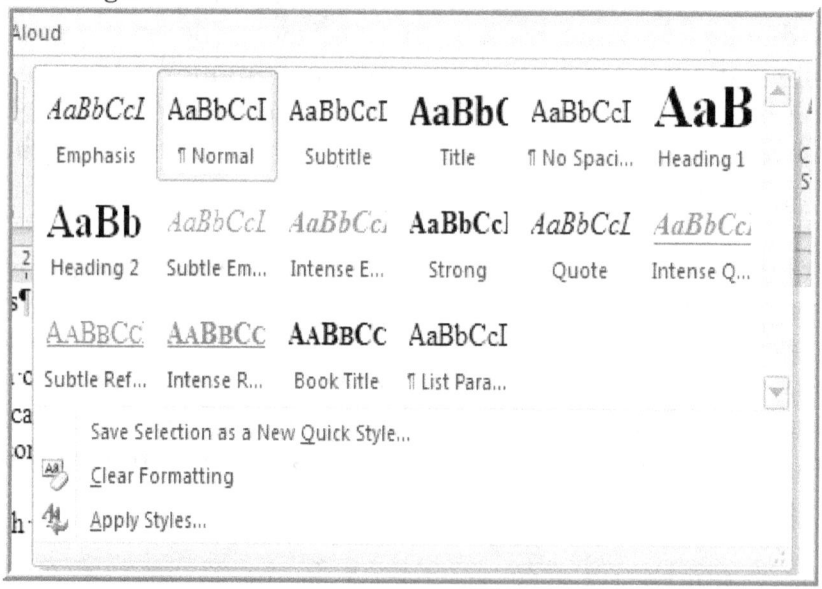

The Normal option is the main text of a page. Each paragraph you type is normal by default. In this chapter, we'll be focusing on Heading 1 – 3.

A chapter title should always be set to Heading 1. Subtopics should be heading 2 or 3. The lower the number, the larger the text. Below is an example:

Growing Potatoes → Heading 1 - chapter name

Normal text paragraph

Preparing the soil ———→ Heading 2 - Subtopic

Normal text paragraph

Types of Potatoes ———→ Heading 2 - Subtopic

Normal text paragraph

Sweet Potatoes ——— Heading 3 - Subtopic of 'Types of Potatoes

Normal text paragraph

Irish Potatoes ——————→ Heading 3 - Subtopic of 'Types of Potatoes'

Normal text paragraph

If the above example was the complete content of the book, it would produce one of the following tables of contents:

Contents

The first example creates a table with all three headings. Heading 1 is the chapter, heading 2 is the subtopic under heading 1, and heading 3 is the subtopic under heading 2. Decide which format is best for your book, and choose the depth of your table of contents when you insert it.

When formatting my book, I always use headings to indicate a topic or subtopic – even if I don't plan to use them in a table of contents. It makes formatting easier and more consistent.

To insert a table of contents, first format all your chapter headings and subtopic headings in your manuscript with the appropriate heading.

Insert a page break right after your title page and make sure the cursor is in that page.

Look at the menu in Word 2010 and click on 'References'. Click on the Table of Contents icon at the upper left. See below:

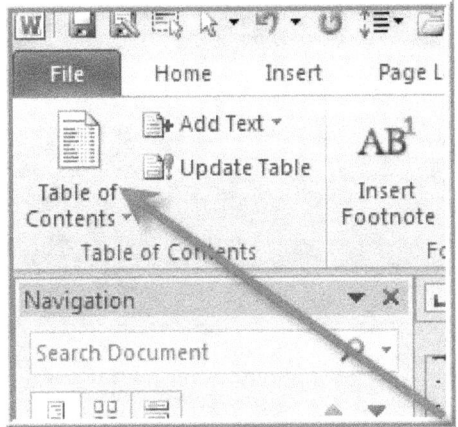

If you plan on using all of your headings in the table, click on **Automatic Table 1**. This will give you a table similar to example 1 above.

If you only want to use heading 1 or 1 and 2, click on **'Insert Table of Contents'** at the bottom of the drop down menu. See below:

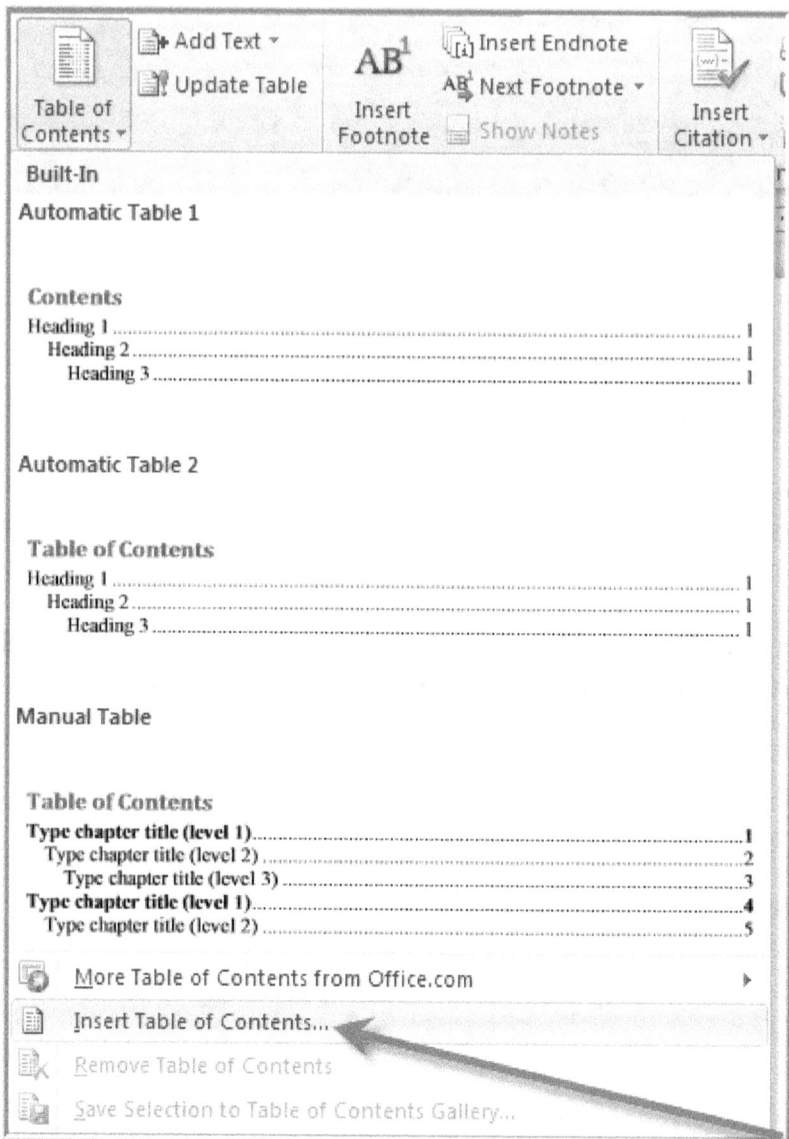

Choose the number of levels. See below:

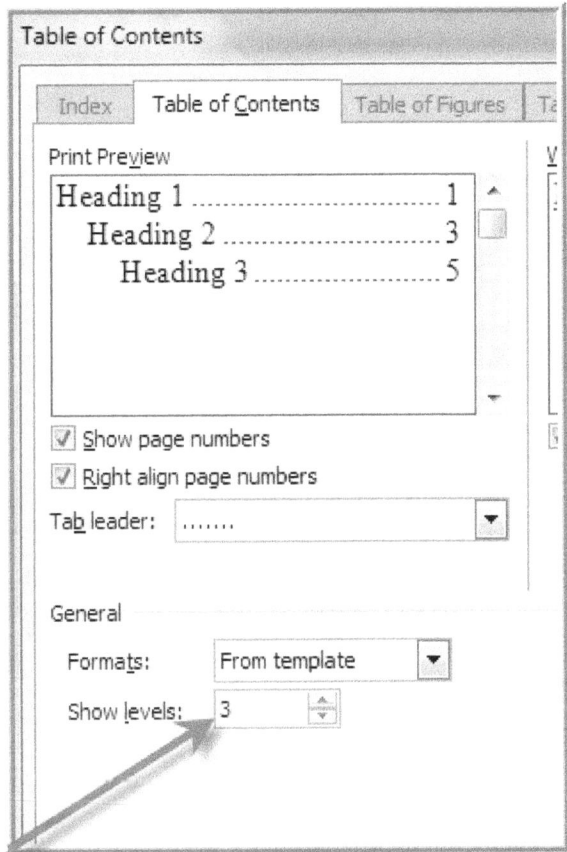

3 will show headings 1 through 3. Choose the level that fits your book.

Note: If you have trouble finding a heading, you can use a shortcut. For example, if you want to turn a line of text into heading 3, but Word only shows up to heading 2, press **Ctrl-Alt-3**. This will create heading 3. This shortcut will also work with heading 1 and 2.

Here is an example from my current book. Since the topics are clear from the chapter titles, I only have one level.

Table of Contents

The Table of Contents is not dynamic, but it can be updated easily. Any time you add text, change the page lay outs, or do anything that might change the page numbers or headings, update the table of contents. Simply put your cursor over the table, right-click, and choose '**Update Field**'. When the window pops up, choose to update the entire table. That way Word will import any headings you have added as well as update the page numbers.

Setting up the Page Layout.

There are a few things to consider when choosing a page layout. The first and most obvious is the size of the book you plan to use. If you are going to be using CreateSpace or Lightning Source, check out the standard layouts they accept. I highly recommend staying with common book sizes. The most common size for most book types is 6x9. That's 6 inches wide by 9 inches long. Most printers (including CreateSpace and Lightning Source) accept 6x9 books.

The margin is the next decision you need to make. For the best results, try to stay between 1 inch and ½ an inch. I prefer to use ¾ of an inch (0.75) for my margins. This allows me to print my header at ½ an inch and maintain a nice look.

The header and footer text will print outside of the main text area, so these margins must be smaller than the text margins. For example, if you set your page margins for .75, then you will need your header and footer margins to be smaller. Maybe something like .5. If they were the same setting, the footer would print on top of the page text. If they are too close, it will look like a misprint or part of the page text. I recommend keeping the headers and footers at least .25 (1/4 of an inch) away from the page margin.

If a margin page is too narrow, the printed text will show up in the gutter of the book. This is the area near the book's binding.

Line Spacing

When submitting a manuscript to agents or editors, the standard formatting is double-spaced lines. This may be the standard for evaluating manuscripts, but it is not the standard for printing a book. Double-spaced lines do not look good in print.

There are a lot of line spacing options, but this instruction is intended as a quick reference for the most common book types. I recommend changing the line spacing to 1.0. If the lines look crunched together, you can manually set it to 1.15 or something similar. To set this option, highlight the entire document, or if you want to exclude the title page, place your cursor in front of the first letter of chapter one, and then press Ctrl-Shift-End. This will take you to the bottom of the manuscript and highlight all the text from chapter one until the end.

From the Home tab, click on the drop-down arrow beside the line spacing icon. See below:

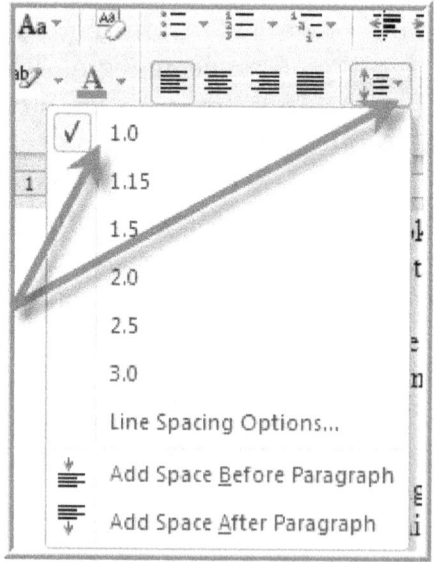

1.0 looks good for most books. You can also click Line Spacing Options and manually adjust it to your liking.

Orphans

An orphan is a word or line of text that is left hanging by itself. In a printed book, this can be very unattractive. You don't want to have the last few words of a chapter sitting alone on a page. Usually orphan control is enabled by default, but to make sure it's turned on, do the following.

Place your cursor anywhere in a body of a normal text paragraph. Make sure the Home tab is selected, and click the expansion button under Paragraph. See below:

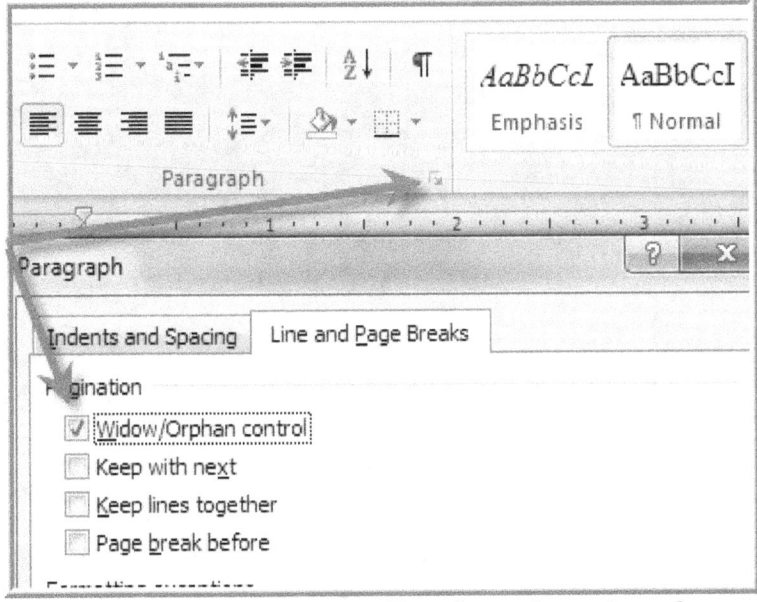

Go to the Line and Page Breaks tab and make sure the Window/Orphan Control is checked.

Setting the Page Layout

Most of Word's templates are designed for paper sizes used in office environments. This doesn't work for book printing. We must select a layout that fits our book size. The easiest set up is to use the custom size option. To access this, click on the Page Layout tab in word and then click the expansion icon at the bottom right of the Page Setup menu.

Click the Paper tab.

Under the Paper size, click the drop down arrow, and then scroll down to Custom size.

Change the Width to 6

Change the Height to 9

Change Apply to: Whole Document

See below:

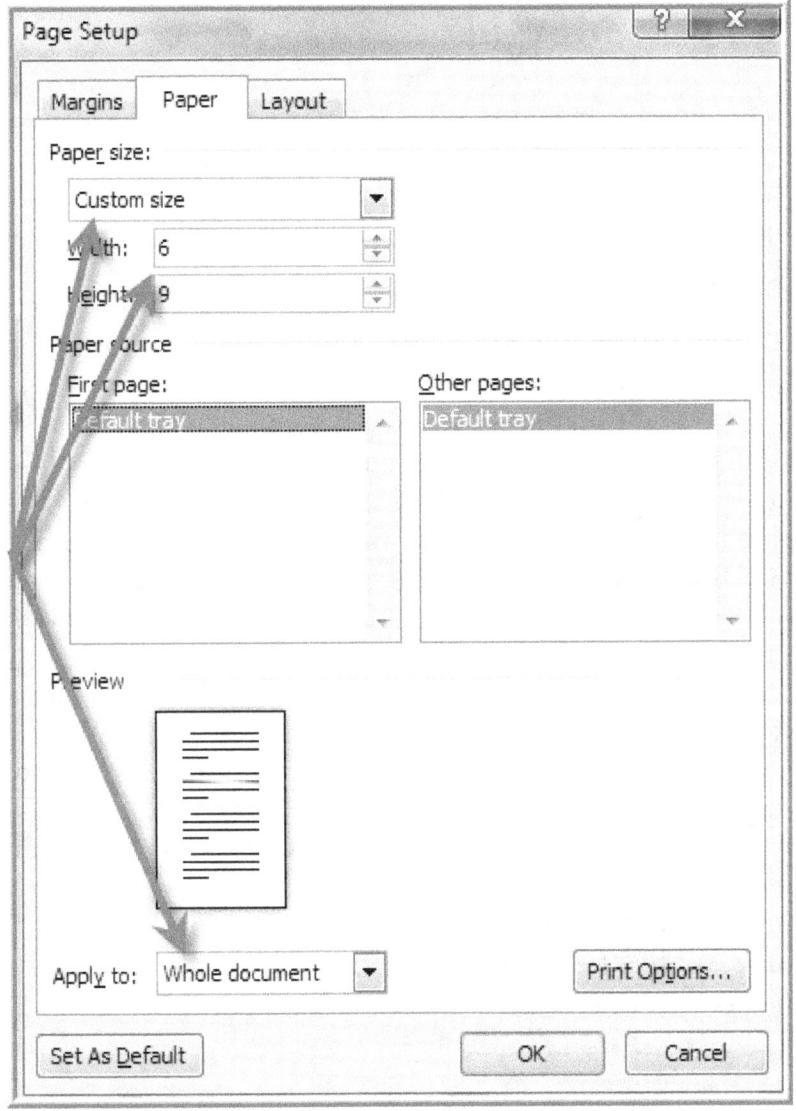

Once applied, the entire document will shrink to 6x9 and the page count will be renumbered. If you already have a table of contents, you will need to update it. Right click on the table and select update field, then click to update entire table.

Setting the Margins

The look of the margins of a book is up to the author's preference, but these are the measurements I use in my books. As stated earlier, you must consider the gutter of the page, header and footer, and one other thing – trimming.

Trimming is what the printer does after printing the book. The pages are squared off for a perfect fit, and though modern technology can get close, there is always excess paper printed and then cut away. If text runs close to the edge of the page, there is a chance the text could be trimmed away. Or the text could end up too close to the edge of the page and look amaturish. The settings I'll use here create a safe distance for all the variables of printing.

From the Page Layout tab, Click on Margins and choose **Custom Margins** from the bottom of the dropdown.

Change the top, bottom, left, and right margins to .75. This is ¾ of an inch.

Make sure the orientation is in portrait mode – unless you have a reason to print in landscape.

The gutter should be 0, and the gutter position Left.

Change Applies to: **Whole Document**.

See below for an example.

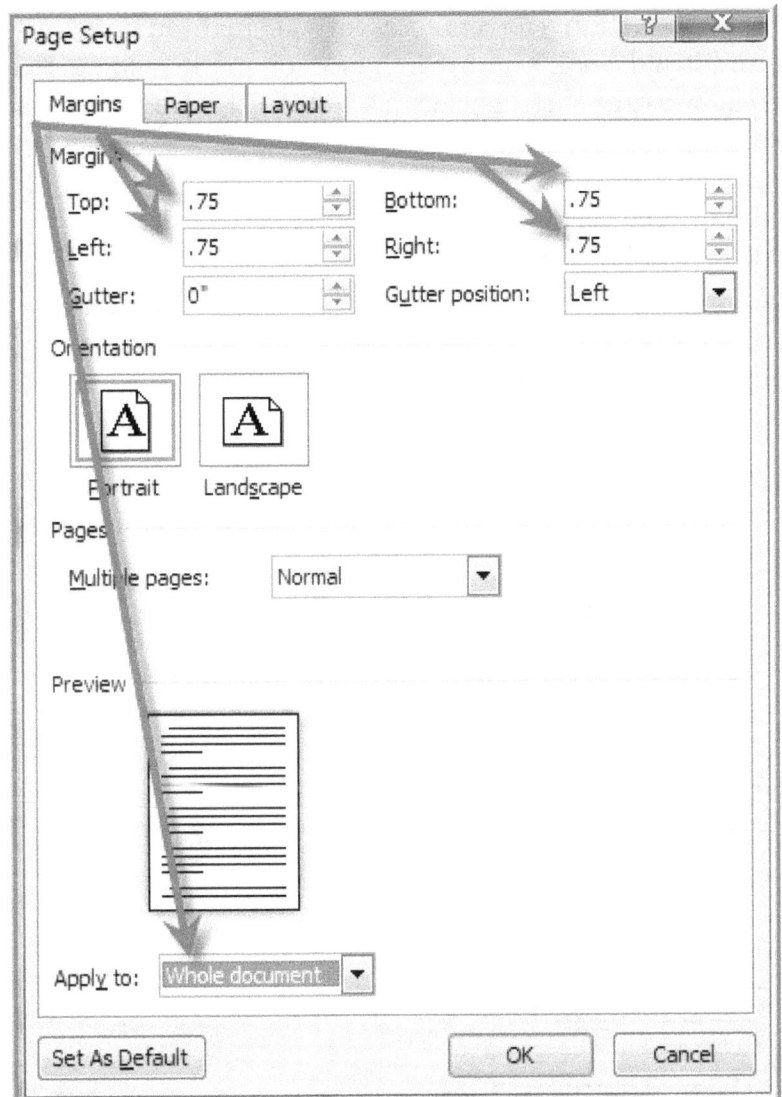

Feel free to adjust this to your taste, but stay away from the edge of the page, gutter, and the headers and footers.

Header and Footer Layout

The headers and footers are measured from the edge of the page. As stated earlier, the distance from the edge has

to be smaller than the margins of the printed text. Too close and it will look amateurish or even print incorrectly. From the Margin settings setup, click on the **Layout** tab. Change the Header to .5
Change the Footer to .5
Change applies to: **Whole Document**
See the example below:

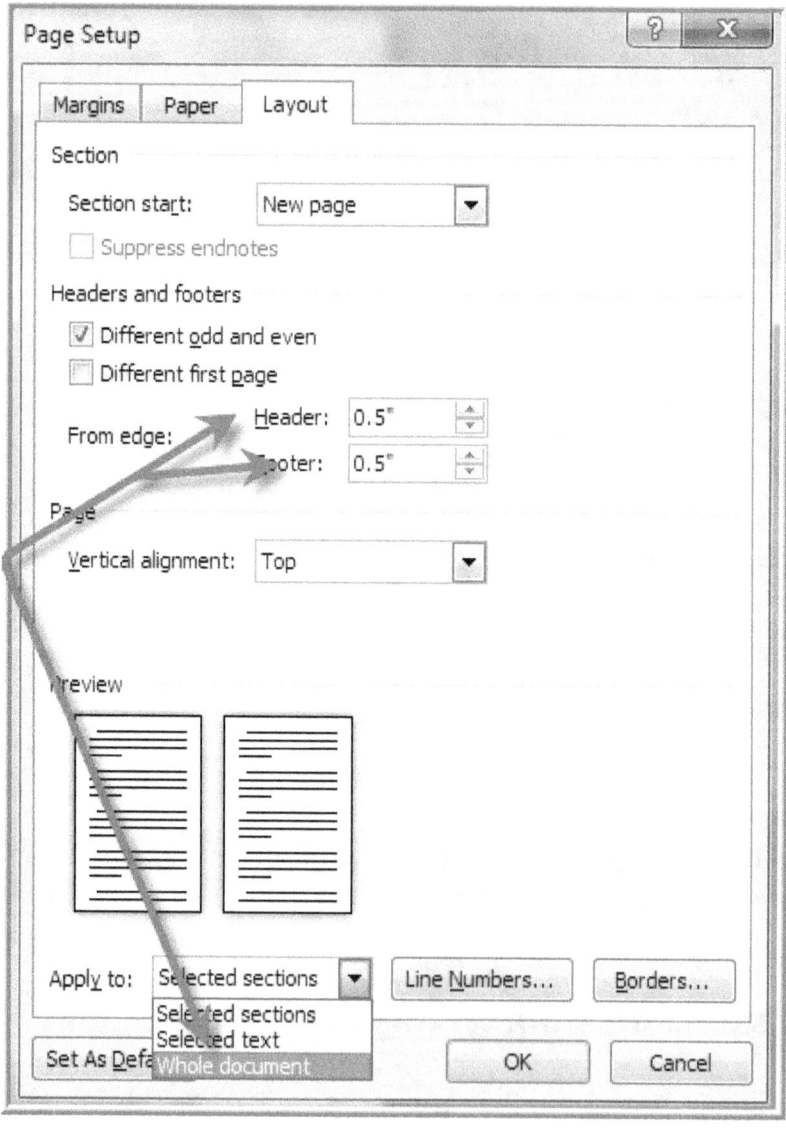

The header and footer do not have to be the same, but in most cases, it looks more semetrical and creates a professional appearance. You may want to experiment and see what looks best for your style of book.

This example book doesn't use headers, but I've included them so that readers who use headers will have these settings.

Saving Your Manuscript for Publication

Most presses require a manuscript to be in PDF format. Most Word versions can export a document to PDF. The most important thing is to embed your fonts into the word document. For normal documents, don't embed fonts since this will bloat your file size, but for the file you'll be uploading, the font should always be embedded.

If the font isn't found on the printer's system, it will substitute a compatible font. This takes away your control of the look and feel of your book. A slightly different font can dramatically change your layout, leaving sloppy formatting or changing your page numbers.

Embedding fonts takes a few steps. First go to File, Options, and click Save.
At the bottom of the window, click on Embed Fonts in the file. See below:

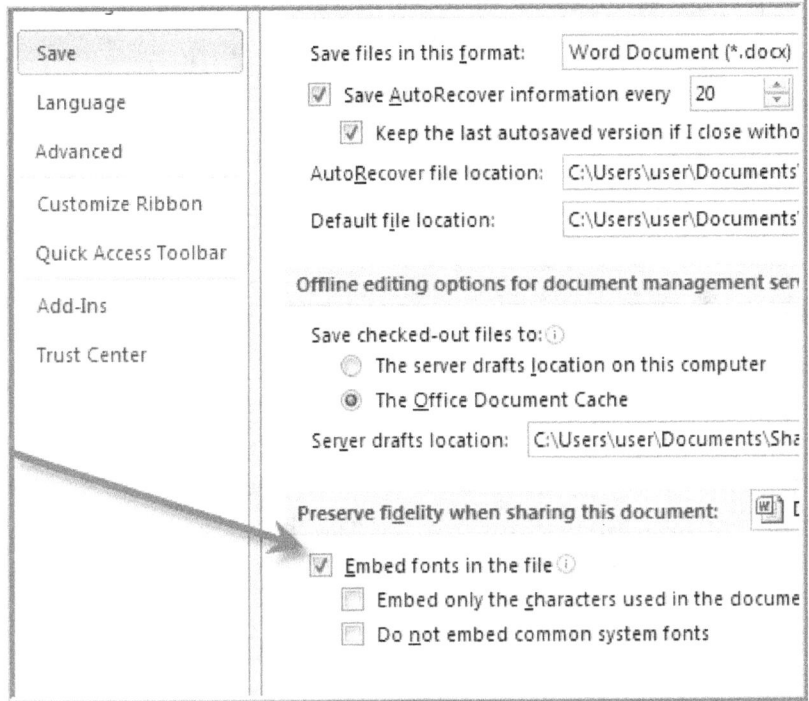

At this point, it's a good idea to save the document. I like to identify the document by using a filename like MyBookTitle-embedded.doc. This way if changes need to be made, the fonts won't be inadvertently left out in the next revision.

The next step is to save the document as a PDF file. This will create another separate file. Click on File, Save As, click the dropdown arrow beside Save as Type:. Choose PDF.

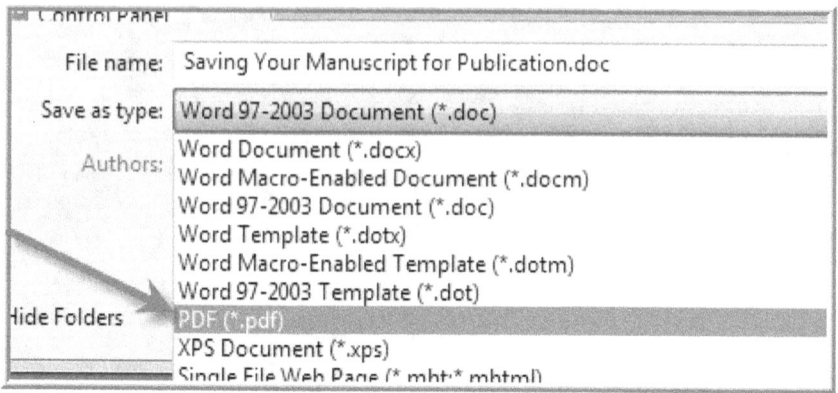

Before saving, make sure you have the radio button selected beside Standard, and then click Options.

From the options window, check the box beside 'ISO 19005-1 compliant. See below:

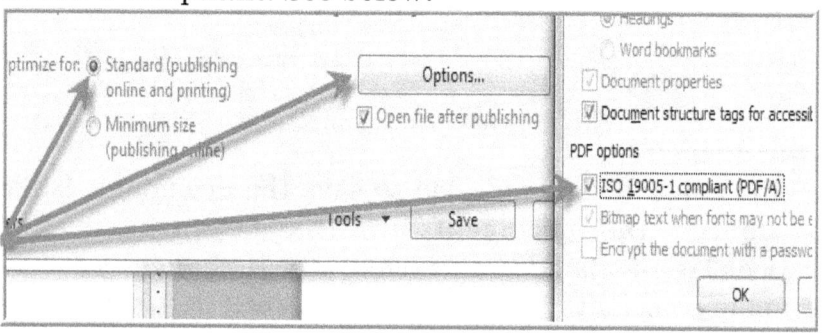

Click okay and save the pdf file.

Important Note: If you have a pdf plugin set up as a printer, don't print to PDF. Doing so will not embed the fonts into the document.

Once you save, your document is complete and ready to be uploaded to the printing service you are using. This process will work with CreateSpace, Lulu, Lightning Source, and many other popular presses. Verify with your printing service to see if other special requirements are necessary for their systems.

42

Saving for the Kindle

If you are planning to publish directly to amazon through kdp.amazon.com, you are already prepared to complete your kindle document. KDP requests documents be saved in an html format.

Go back to your embedded Word document. Click on Save As, click the dropdown arrow, and choose 'Web Page, Filtered'. See below:

File name:	Saving Your Manuscript for Publication.doc
Save as type:	Word 97-2003 Document (*.doc)

Word Document (*.docx)
Word Macro-Enabled Document (*.docm)
Word 97-2003 Document (*.doc)
Word Template (*.dotx)
Word Macro-Enabled Template (*.dotm)
Word 97-2003 Template (*.dot)
PDF (*.pdf)
XPS Document (*.xps)
Single File Web Page (*.mht;*.mhtml)
Web Page (*.htm;*.html)
Web Page, Filtered (*.htm;*.html)
Rich Text Format (*.rtf)
Plain Text (*.txt)
Word XML Document (*.xml)
Word 2003 XML Document (*.xml)
OpenDocument Text (*.odt)
Works 6 - 9 Document (*.wps)

This option creates a subfolder for images and attachments, so I recommend saving this document to its own folder.

There are other ways to prepare a document for uploading to Kindle, but this is by far the easiest. It compiles everything into a single page. Now all that is left is uploading to the kdp direct publishing site. Point to this file for the upload and the site will pull any attachments or pictures.

Congratulations! When you finish these steps, your manuscripts are fully publishable and ready for printing.

Thank You

I appreciate your support for this book. It is my hope that the information I've put in this book was helpful in your publishing needs. Independent authoring and partnership printing is a trend still in its infancy. Many authors are paying hundreds of dollars or more to get their manuscripts typeset. I hope this book has saved you time and money.

If you enjoyed this book, please rate this book on Amazon.com. Also check out other books by this author at http://www.amazon.com/Eddie-Snipes/e/B005IYF3DW/ref=eddiesnipesco-20

www.ingramcontent.com/pod-product-compliance
Lightning Source LLC
Chambersburg PA
CBHW070235290526
45789CB00004B/1640